Morning Light

First published in 1998 by
Slow Dancer Press
59 Parliament Hill London NW3 2TB
England

British Library Cataloguing-in-Publication Data. A catalogue record
for this book is available from The British Library.

ISBN 1 871033 41 1

Slow Dancer poetry titles are available in the U.K. through Signature Book
Representation distributed by Littlehampton Book Services and in the U.S.A. &
Canada through Dufour Editions, PO Box 7, Chester Springs, PA 19425 0007.

Cover design: Keenan

Slow Dancer Logo: East Orange

Printed in Great Britain by Peepal Tree Press
I 7 King's Avenue, Leeds LS6 1QS

This book is set in Elegant Garamond 10/13.

Slow Dancer Press

Morning Light

Lee Harwood

Slow Dancer Press

Acknowledgements

Some of these poems first appeared in: *Ambit, Blue Cage, Cafe Review, Exact Change Yearbook, Giants Play Well in The Drizzle, Grand Street, Grille, James White Review, Lift, New American Writing, Nineties Poetry, Oasis, Poesie Europe, Shearsman, Slow Dancer, Tears in the Fence, Under Surveillance, Yellow Crane.*

'Dreams of Armenia' was published, in a Romanian translation by Virgil Mihaiu, in *Ararat* (Bucharest) and *Arca* (Arad).

'African Violets' was included in the anthology **The Long Pale Corridor: Contemporary Poems of Bereavement** edited by Judi Benson and Agneta Falk (Bloodaxe Books); 'Air Clamps' in **The Poetry Book Society Anthology** 2 edited by Anne Stevenson (Hutchinson); 'Czech Dream' in **The Six Towns Poetry Festival Anthology**, 1992, 'Days and Nights' in the **1995 Festival Anthology** and six other poems in the **1996 Festival Anthology/Etruscan Books reader 6**, all edited by Nicholas Johnson; 'Homage to Albert Ryder and Bill Corbett' in **Of Eros and Dust: Poems from the City** edited by Steve Anthony (The Oscars Press); 'The Old Question' and part of 'Summer 1993' in **Jugular Defences: An AIDS Anthology** edited by Peter Daniels and Steve Anthony (The Oscars Press).

'The Songs of Those Who Are on the Sea of Glass.' appeared as a very limited edition pamphlet from Short Run, Cheltenham.

My thanks to all these editors and publishers.

Lee Harwood, 1998

Contents

Gilded White

for Sandy Berrigan

the snow is deep and soft on the steps
the temple roof thickly cloaked in snow
trees heavy with it
the gold carvings and red beams
luminous in the muted winter light

I look down on this from a high window
beside the window stands a tall grey feather
trimmed with charms   your gift
hung with small bells and beads and a moon
softly wrapped in wool

the day may turn   a soft dull light
to a brightness   a yellow glitter in the snow
a white cloud in a corner of the window
the ghost of a half moon in the sky

a table, a lamp, some books, a radio,
the sound of the sea in the background.
a quiet day. a cup of coffee.

on the snow covered path
or a street in a city miles away
a stillness. a middle aged woman pauses by the arch
and knocks snow from her shoes
an old man stands erect at the entrance to Via Orfeo
his cheap shirt washed ironed and neatly buttoned

Japan is a long way away   Italy is a long way away
California is a long way away   Sussex is a long way away
but all gently wrapped together in this moment
your gift

Homage to Albert Ryder
and Bill Corbett 1990

A full moon behind a moving veil of clouds
in a silver black marbled sky.
And below -
the yellow lights from a few windows,
people noisily walking home,
talking loudly, laughing,
but all in a near silence that envelops
a clock's tick, a passing car,
a telephone ringing in the next building.

The moon darkens as the clouds mass.

*

In my room a flickering candle
illuminates the ikon,
the Christ in silver,
his mother and saints in gold.
A thick soft darkness.

*

Then the moon comes almost clear
illuminating the sky, giving a pale
ochre tint to the surrounding clouds,
silvering the wave crests out across the sea,
and the still ponds in dark fields.

As though a crazed skin covers our eyes
beyond which we see some form of stillness.

October Night

"asleep among appearances" Octavio Paz

Strange world.
The warbling and ringing of car and shop alarms
                                    in the street,
shadows on the ceiling.
A large mauve head appearing in an ochre background.
As though a dream landscape but not.
As though a painting but not.

Eyes shut
"you were in another day"
off in the distant mountains
where the darkness breathes
and the black silhouette of a hillside
edges a charcoal grey sky.
A seeming solidity, though thin as paper.

A near astonishment at the "facts",
the surrounding sounds and sights.
The "what is this?", "who is... ?".
No step back possible

But a step towards?   out?

Behind your grey eyes..   These surfaces

A watchfulness, the distance between,
all words probing towards this puzzle.
The possible bridges?   in a clash of dreams -
though that too poetic and abstract to grasp,
shake with your hands.

A past "real", memories haunting amongst reality;
the present so... ?   dazed?   startled?

The colours of the dim light
projected through blinds onto a ceiling,
the feel of a cotton pillowcase on my cheek
And beyond that?

Not avoiding thought by a fence of questions,
but somehow unable...   to move

Clinging onto the rock face
The rain beating on the skylight
Clipped on
Floating like a sleeping angel
who then wakes touching the softness below

The Old Question

for Ben Watkins

The stillness,
is that what it's about?
The glint of light in a glass
set on a round wood table?
Sun streaming in from the window
onto some papers, a moving hand,
a man's knee.
That moment, stood still it seems,
a small heaven,
but outside as surely the wind
tugs at a tree, people walk by in the street
going various places.
What to do with this?
Take it while it's there, but... ?
"Moving through time" an unreal phrase,
but with an edge to it.
Stumbling often enough,
clasping such precious minutes
like icons to our breasts.
Somehow to.....   What?
Somehow to negotiate or navigate or
just steer clear headed
through the days?
I don't know. I get up
and walk across the room,
turn and

Days and Nights : Accidental Sightings
A bundle of 50 sticks for Joseph Cornell and others

a wire bent round a corner

*

So many pebbles on the beach, uncountable.

*

a silver fish reeled in from the sea.   the sun glinting.

*

the line that says nothing. A chair creaks.

*

cut wood. walk the streets at night. rock'n'roll.

*

the wind.

*

fierce gusts of rain following into the night.

*

wind whistling and moaning around the house

*

stuck in the fact of absence

*

the air lightens - suddenly a blue sky, small white clouds
masking the sun.

*

the pale ochre, wheat white grass as autumn clears its way and
the rust red patches on the moor

*

In the town...

*

Making the bridges

*

... walking upstairs carrying a basket of wet clothes...

*

the wind ruffling the water of a small pond

*

the clarity of sunlight, the calm it brings, inside not outside.

*

on the cliff top

*

...warm from a bath... scented... simple luxuries...
in the night

*

a clock ticks. a silence of sorts.

*

late afternoon - coming round a corner, down a hill - the sudden
sight of a grey silk sea shining

*

towards dusk two kingfishers skimming the river
walk on and back to a town

*

that's it

*﹚

And now...

*

(space)

*

Watching clouds through a barred window passing from the west.
White clouds   blue sky.

*

always in the present?   ing   ing

*

Where else?   or some lack of imagination?

*

a lot of anger.   a lot of death-wish.

*

"Our beards stiff with ice" - that's a memory.
(I live in a version of the past as well that can be measured
in minutes - not just the present.)

*

Other people somewhere come into this world.

*

music on the radio

*

Walk through the words.

*

the memory of a totally perfect day near indescribable - a time
of such joys and deep happiness.

*

And then out the door into a fine drizzle.

*

As Tom once wrote "this trick doesn't work."
But what trick?   A need to...
but what/why?   and who cares?
"Better than hanging 'round street corners," said Mother Oppen.
Really?

*

These words can rest here on the page, whilst dust slowly coats
the plates. A cupboard of dishes rarely used.
Grandmothers as icons.

*

Who needs it?

*

Out to sea the continually changing horizon
the qualities of light
from left to right   east to west
a startling clarity, a rain storm, more clarity shading into a
haze, a mist. Moving all the time.
And the colours?! A whole book on the colours.

*

sullen

*

Grey dark clouds, continual rain.

*

the alignment of stars

*

bare branches.

*

chalk white boxes.

*

This could go on a long time, but won't.

*

the word is...   A dressing gown hung on the door.
A quietness in the house
Clock ticks   Sound of light rain falling,
dripping from the window sill.

*

clear headed

*

Distant sounds - waves breaking on the beach, traffic a street
away.

*

Bright star maps - Orion's Belt over the ploughed fields. Following
the muddy path, crossing the swollen stream, in darkness,...

*

a blue sky. spring coming. 8.00 a.m. on the beach. sun shining.

*

The white box contains a landscape - bare branches, a night sky
set with stars, a window, a figure, curious objects.
We look in from the outside.

Magnetic Pull

A bruised night sky
muffling a full moon

that pulls out the unreason
the craziness from heads

so that wandering in rooms
and streets   people who don't know

what   but fall on...
along some zigzag path

preying on and preyed upon
half blind in the half light

behind which pulses 'The Magnet'
"the mist monster" you say

"headstrong" you say
sliding into fitful sleep

lost into nightmares
of mothers and daughters

and pulled up out again
into an awake night

moonlight filling the room
the empty seafront promenade

staggering zombies or sleepwalkers
silently crash through air barriers

a small object is set on a table
the faint light catches one side of it

Moon Watching: 7 nights

1st Night:

the light of the full moon
cuts across
my bed
my bare shoulder
silver white
summer night

2nd Night:

the moonlit sea like old silver
rolling across an ikon

3rd Night:

but

full moon:
  "leave the phone alone
    don't negotiate or make decisions
    till it's passed"
said an oracle or a
wise woman or a smart woman
to me some years ago

4th Night:

yet

the moon so clear and bright
worshipped or feared
both

a presence
a cold pure white
above the town   above the sea
cutting down   (all to size?)

month after month this
strange power or "fascination"
no answer to the "why"

an awed muddle? when you step back?
and then get on with the "business"

but a passing glimpse
as you climb the stairs
or walk by a window

5th Night:

inland veiled moonlight
is caught on the still pond
two shafts of light fork
down on the dark fields and hills
briefly as the clouds loosen and shift

we plod on through the darkness

6th Night:

a solitary and remote obsession it seems
but joined in silence,
singular to plural, on occasion, we

thin words   thin light

7th Night:

> And in the East they had parties
> to do this same thing, so I hear
> A platform built out on a lake
> wine and instruments and poetry
> to accompany the moon watch

Summer 1990

Swimming at night,
the creamy full summer moon
gilding the dark lacquered sea.
Floating in the soft swell of the waves
as though suspended...
the sea soft and warm
as a lover's skin, near heaven,
only better.

What next?

I wade out of the sea,
dry myself then sit watching
the sea, the moon,
the small lights on the distant pier.
Walk home, go to bed, dreamy
still hung in those waves.
Such precious time given or taken.

Air Clamps

The building is very large that you see
across the fields, dear reader,
can you see, above the green the white
of its walls and red of the tiles?

Standing amongst all this green
whether to sigh in admiration of a vague harmony
or to rage at this fixity? Huh?

A gardener or a visitor might be moving
in the distance towards or away from that building;
or simply standing still musing or about to
step off into some irresolute, even meaningless, action.

I step off into the bushes, the hillsides of long grasses,
the sunken path now overgrown and decorated with orchids,
to emerge later, somewhat sweaty, but pleasantly glowing.

The Stuff is fixed in its grip on us
but we slip loose some times and decay
gradually eats at the structures, we hope.

In 20 years' time the white may be grey,
or still a dazzling white, but the house now
turned into a hotel for conferences, gourmet weekends.
The estate divided, the landscape farmed,
or built on even, though unlikely in this place.

A frazzled reader shoves old postcards, photos,
jigsaw puzzles into a remote drawer
wanting only to get up and out the door
into the street air, but then suddenly
dawns the weirdly controlled clamps rotating
in the sky by unseen hands.

Czech Dream

1.

'The last bell is ringing
The fairy tale is over'
    shout some distant Czechs
    early on a frosty evening

"A sharp new moon
in a smudged pink sky"
the story begins,
but seemed a repeated story
heard too many times before.
That tale over,
but another continues?

    "Arm in arm with you"?

2.

The story began

    "Waking at five and passing into a jumble
    of dreams that with time ended by
    taking me into your arms.

    Over the weeks apart our minds race
    ahead of our bodies.
    When we meet, when they catch up,
    then like a golden light, yes?
    descends upon us wholly.

The dream is right.
The words wrong-foot sometimes
but try to push through the briars,
leap over them sometimes,
Brer Rabbit and all."

But I built too much in those dreams?
Too many scars and losses behind us.
Yet this chance, come upon by accident,
precious but shakey.

3.

Not the village wedding,   the mad bride's suicide,
billowing white veils against the greenery
of leaves or water

but

      "The thought of being with you.
      Dizzy floating I bite my lip
      in the middle of 'worldly commerce'."

4.

"'God has many mansions' said Miss Flanagan S.R.N.
and the mansion where we dwelt...
'and which mansion did you sleep in?' she added
                        with a sly laugh
The rosaries and mugs of sherry are duly told
Our love stained sheets tell
our mansion"

5.

Yet it doesn't shelter us
stave off the unavoidable collapse.
Dreams and stories snare us
before we can get past rubbing our eyes.
A mess of fears sets in that neither
Venus nor Ganymede can dispel.
Like Cupid a blind romantic rush
tips us sprawling into a mirrored room
where self-absorbed dreamers wander
almost ghostlike.
The creators of such illusions
stand close beside us. The creatures.

6.

Spoken into a mirror

"I travel to you

your warmth
To stand or lie in each other's arms

battle scars, tired of the old deceits
we come nervously to each other
yet surely (we think)

Is this the clarity
we dream of?

Not magic but more powerful
in its simplicity -
us

Guided out beyond the ramparts
the savage boors

Touch me   you"

and tinkling bells in the distance
and the words flatter themselves, words on words,
and the first flakes of snow falling softly,
the landscape whitening out

African Violets

for Pansy Harwood
my grandmother 1896-1989

Flags stream from the tops of the silver pyramids
Purple flowers present themselves to the air, the world
Chopin fights his way through all the notes, the choices

All this, and yet that emptiness

A real heart-breaker, tears in my eyes

What did I give you? At the last a pot of flowers,
your favourite colour, you said
then died soon after, the day after
I'd left you there in the bare hospital room
your eyes and voice so clear in the recognition
like so many years before   "O Travers"

And you gave me? everything I know.

But to reduce this to yet another poem
to entertain

pages of words creating old routines

I systematically smash all those pretty pictures,
they won't do anymore.
"That was a bit unnecessary, son," you say.
I know, but their weight does you no service.

My blood is your blood,
it's as ancient as that;
pride and style that you had,
and with all a lovely generosity
I treasure.

I find myself moving as you would,
not the same but similar,
sharing your tastes and paths;
the night jasmine bower.

The strength of these memories
The comfort your home was

Yet it seems almost another world -
building rabbit hutches on winter evenings
in your living room, sawdust and
wood shavings on the worn carpet, easily cleared.
A house that was lived in, not exhibited.

And all those other evenings, summer or winter,
spent pickling onions, or bottling fruit,
or wrapping boxes of apples for store,
or stringing onions to hang in the shed
above the sacked potatoes,
or mending our own shoes,
all the work, cooking, making,
fixing, all done capably, easily
together.

But you now gone forever

Not sat in the corner of the couch
after your morning bath, with a cup of tea
reading the morning paper.
That ritual finished

though other "stuff" continues
as your blood continues to flow in me
no matter what I might say
(the tense continually shifts, past and present blur)
we both love(d) love and were, are natural liars,
easy with the "truth", turning facts to meet the story;
we both have a distaste for "trade" -
all the contradictions happily ignored;
we both...

Now wandering helpless around my room
the rich world about,
the flags and skies, the dreams

I talk to you again and again,
I see you again and again   sat there

Tao - yun meets Sandy Berrigan *

A wall hung with charms -
pictures, a Welsh love-spoon, beads
"for worrys"

I live with this
the touchstones, rituals, to hold off or hold to...
Clinging to the walls?

A soft hot night, and May
now, a half moon so clear
in the dark sky

All round the globe
Like Chinese poems of dear friends' separations,
brief meetings, then parting again

Shifts and changes
that can't be charmed away
only soothed by this "hollow"

I remember the taste of coffee
as late at night I entered a room
where you lay sleeping

*"Tao-yun (c400 A.D.), (poet and) wife of General Wang Nin-chih.
The general was so stupid that she finally deserted him."
Arthur Waley - **170 Chinese Poems.**

Summer 1993

early in the evening
the smell of jasmine

pushes death away

in the fading light
a strong wind tugs across the sea
bright white crests on the waves

my son enters pushing his bike
my daughter runs downstairs

pushes death away

*

slid into a selfish gloom
the result of... ?
An overcast summer's day by the sea,
luminous grey white clouds,
patches of bright sunshine,
but a dullness in one's heart,
if not elsewhere?
At that age...
At some point in one's life
when...   what does it matter?

The losses irreparable, irreplaceable.
The deaths of loved ones,
and one's own death hovering nearby
that would seem welcome but for...
the loved ones living and those moments
when a flower's scent or a shaft of sunlight...

*

But as though out on one's own, almost.
"The solitary" - though that too dramatic.
"The melancholic" - self-absorbed romancing
that has a sharp edge to it,
cuts deeper than your finger.

And you who reads this -
it must bore you or seem so irrelevant.
I need to write this for whatever reason
but you don't need to read it. (goodbye)

Inside the castle all's well.
Outside the angry creatures
pounce and flail
in swirling mists or black night.
Dreams horribly real.

*

changes in the past, but ahead?
Drilled into the ground
stuck waiting
the light fading,
or "dormant" some say
depending on one's cheer (glad or no).

*

surviving, not perkily ending.

just to get it over.

over the blue grey hills
angels hover in a paleing sky
still-faced   shadows cross a face
eyelash flicker   bright sunlight
such gloom?   foolish but...
step back   still spot

In the Mountains

In memory of Paul Evans

A bright full moon
in a clear black sky
over Llyn Ogwen.

Eight years pass.
A climber falls.

Now where's that leave us?

A veiled smoky moon
on a dark night,
the lake a dense black.

Absence gnawed at.
Stuck in a cleft.

A car drives by far below.
Some people returning somewhere.

Later - a chill dull day.
Jagged blocks and spikes
pump the heart heat.
Haul up through rock
onto snow covered ridge.

Did it.   Do it.   Then... ?

Then strapping on crampons
and on up - as we'd both do -
on up. Yes, magnificent.

A rose red gold sun in ice air.

"Where's Mr. Perky Now?"

Days and nights pass
and the weight increases,
steadily pressing down.
Deaths and losses,
wrong doing, facts,
without forgiveness.
A lead cloak around your shoulders.
So tired.

What's done "is done"
and that no excuse.
Guilt and grief bound in
to the fabric, it seems forever.

Enough said. "Stop it."
The words, the talking.

And living with all this.

The glimmer of sunlight
early in the morning.

Hard to believe
anything's final, but...

A white terrace of houses
up from the sea
where people live in rooms
once loved by others.
The little empires we build.

A faint dream, seasons passed, and
swimming through glittering waves
while a man walks by to start
another night shift.

Dreams of Armenia

like an angel of death
telling the tale again and again
never any release

the dry rustle of feathers
behind your ear
a feather brushing your neck, your cheek

then a silence
a shadow traveller
then it starts again

*

1894 August: Sasun and surrounding villages attacked by Turks and Kurds. 3,000 Armenians slaughtered. "The Armenians were absolutely hunted like wild beasts," said H.S. Shipley, British representative.

1895: Ottoman sultan puts into effect his "final solution" for the Armenian "problems". Special army units are formed. 30,000 Armenians murdered and over 8,000 flee the country.

1896, 26-27 August: In Constantinople 6,000 murdered, the rest flee.

1896, 15-17 September: In Eghin 2,000 murdered.

1908: "Young Turks" massacre 15,000 in Adana, and 15 to 25 thousand in the surrounding villages. "Conservative estimates," say the consuls of the "Great Powers".

1915-16: One and a half million Turkish Armenians murdered out of a population of three million.

The lists and details continue and continue, the facts of numberless horrors pile up endlessly like torn bodies in the Kemakh gorge.

*

In a dream a door opens
the long dead father stands there
Many others come and go
A friend enters and stays there
fixed there   the light streaming
past his silhouette   the silver edge
a bright day outside

*

If these the last words written,
words then a death, or a silence,
let them at least praise . . .
the "Armenia" I imagine?
moonlight filling a room?
Awkward symbols,
painted boards propped
against a crumbling wall.

*

Komitas the composer silent for 20 years after watching the butchery, the
massacres in a wild and empty place - neither word nor note until his death (in
Paris 1935).

*

a wooden table tilted in the courtyard
an empty glass and coffee cup on one side
the heavy scent of jasmine as the evening . . .

*

Like an Armenian song that tears your heart,
like an Armenian song that tears your heart
with "memories", past loves, empty plains,
empty villages, desolate highlands, clogged ravines.

All those "things" beyond any words.

*

carved stone churches like lighthouses

And in the year 301 A.D. St. Gregory the Illuminator converted
Armenia, the first Christian kingdom in the known world.

Be praised.

And later, in 874, Princess Mariam of Siunia built a nunnery on an island in
Lake Sevan. A place to meet her fisherman lover, they say.

Be praised.

All of Armenia a massive rockbound island rising out of the surrounding plains.
A light to be praised. An illuminating beauty besieged by barbarism and death,
tides of charred destruction.

*

the silence, though not a silence,
the wind in the trees, the sound of water
somewhere, someone calling, far off,
a brief snatch of bird song nearby,
the wind in the trees, the sound of

As though a trickling – very slowly – away

*

The land still there, the sun in the sky.
The eastern provinces, Russian Armenia, still there, real enough,
crops and music and industries and dancing.
The western provinces, Turkish Armenia, there, though
the people dead or driven away. An emptiness.

*

A carved archway. An elaborately carved tomb
broken in half. Stone cut like lace.
The yellow white of grasses late in summer.

Your long black hair, an occasional grey hair,
your deep brown eyes that churn my heart.
Laughing. To touch your face,
kiss your hands and shoulders.
The poplars sway in the breeze,
their leaves twirl and sparkle silver in the sunlight.
The warmth that melts all reserves.

*

... Mkhitar Heratsi sews the wounds up with silk thread, uses mandragora as an
anaesthetic, shows for the first time (1184) how "fevers", typhoid and malaria,
are infectious, uses music for relief of nervous complaints .... A medieval beacon
.... King Gayik Ardsruni of Vaspurakan builds (915-921) a church on the island
of Aghtamar in Lake Van. The outside walls covered in relief carvings of biblical
scenes. A marvel to see with your own eyes .... The island deserted, its people
long since dead, its churches crumbling, the towers sprouting bushes and trees ...

*

Your smile, a glance caught in the market or on the river
bank. Touching as we leave a building.
The evening stroll begins in Yerevan. Lights come on in the
small outdoor cafes. Talk. The tap of backgammon pieces.
A single man's voice singing singing that gives your
heart trembling wings. Then a skirl of reeds. Oboes, piccolos,
flutes, recorders, lutes, zithers and drums.
In the hot night lying together, your eyes glisten in the
soft half-light. The animal scent of our bodies.

*

fields, meadows and orchards, vineyards and pastures in a
stony land. hard and well worked and watered.
apricots, pomegranates, melons, grapes, wheat, sunflowers,
the sheep grazing. blossom in the trees. roses.

*

Towns, villages, churches, graveyards destroyed.
Let off the leash to murder and plunder.

But the notes, the figures, back then - 1895 -

8 October: Trebizond, 920 killed and 200 in the surrounding villages.

21 October: Erzindjan, 260 killed and 850 in the villages.

25 October: Bitlis, 800 killed.

27 October: Baiburt, "several hundred" killed.

30 October: Erzerum, 350 killed.

1-3 November: In Diyarbekir 1,000 killed and in Arabkir 2,800.

4-9 November: Malatia, 3,000 killed.

10-11 November: Kharput, 500 killed.

28 December: Urfa, 3,000 men, women and children seeking safety in the
                cathedral were shot or burned to death there by Turkish troops.
                "The sickening odour of roasting flesh pervaded the town"
                wrote Consul Fitzmaurice.

*

a silence. a door bangs in the wind.
not a dream.

*

Since the 1880s the Turkish army trained by Germans, and fully reorganised in
1913. Liman von Sanders, the German Inspector General of the Turkish Army,
and Freiherr Hans von Wangenheim, the German ambassador, in 1914 assist
with the "master plan" for the destruction of the Armenians, a planned genocide.

"Who remembers the Armenians?" said Hitler years later as he set on the Jews.

*

Massacres, shootings, bayonetting, hacking, thrown into the Kemakh gorge, thrown into the Black Sea, deportations, forced marches, rape, starvation, robbery. Children, men, women, the old and sick.

*

They would do this to you, my love,
and to our son.
*

A summer breeze in the trees
on the hillside, on the river bank.
But the ghosts sighing,
and the crowding savages

Postscript

1   Arshile Gorky wrote in a letter, 14 February 1944, 'What has the Armenian experience to add to modern life? Sensitivity. That is the main, the unforgettable word that has been engraved in my memory of it. Sensitivity to beauty, sensitivity to sadness and melancholy, sensitivity to the frailty as well as the nobility of life. Sensitivity to mental progress. It is such an important contribution. Sensitivity in the day of dehumanization. There lies our contribution to all art. Our Armenia, the sensitivity of Armenia, its understanding and immense experience of bad and good, of the beautiful and ugly, the dead and living is needed by all the world.'

2   Beside the many books on Armenian history as a whole, the most thorough account of 19th and 20th century history is Christopher J. Walker's *Armenia: The Survival of a Nation* (Croom Helm, London, 1980).

The Songs of Those Who Are On The Sea of Glass*

A hospital room in near silence
Men in beds in varying degrees of pain
A clutter and the colour white
The bright January sun
illuminating. . .
the beige of the building opposite
The arrangement of buildings   so beautiful
Clouds and white puffs of smoke from unseen chimneys
reflected in the black windows

Waking to see this   from on high
across the morning courtyard
It's amazing

*

The bright vision fades

A battered piece is put back
on the game board
whose endlessly complicated contradictory rules
......absurd and with no purpose

The box chipped and coated in dust
Jamaican cigars long gone
into the blue haze

*

Osip Mandelstam calls this earth
"a Godgiven palace" "the happy heaven
...the boundless house in which we live our lives"

*

The living dead plod across the ice to
stare through thick glass walls
"Let me in!"   "Let me out!"

As though floating. Couldn't care less.
Which side.   Outside.   Down there.

The ice window
(that's a metaphor)
Climbing over the bones
(that's a metaphor)
Aquarium walls

Grotesque gawping fish
Nightmare stuff

A new moon high in the sky over the sea

*

Suddenly keeling over
A blur
Dream ambulances, rooms, people, tubes

Back and forth over the river

But love and duty call and pull,
Stoic virtues make it amusing,
the whimpers and begging - a story.

*

Talking in code ?

*

A rawness.   The rediscovered face in the mirror
"I know you?"   Mid-morning.
Washed and shaved
A body stitched and wired together.   The Creature.

"The monster! The monster!" fleeing villagers yell
in black and white Transylvania.

"I don't need, I don't need..."

Emptiness would soothe
A bare room   no clutter

*

The sea was frozen as we approached Esbjerg
the crunch and crack of ice beneath the ferry's bow
as it ploughed on towards a grey line in the whiteness

Inland a fox trotted nervously
across snow-covered fields and streams

The warmth of the cabin bunk, of the den,
of the sun when it breaks through
and, wrapped up, you skim stones across
a small frozen pool in the mountains,
the ricochet ringing, whining,
a high singing.

*

black glass windows
across the courtyard
reflections of clouds, columns of smoke
Bright January sun
a glitter in the air
that fills rooms
(a gold-leaf annunciation)

As though reborn
not racked with loss, past if-onlys
To walk at ease with the ghosts
(not a club member yet)
warm and open and thankful

with care
it seems possible

sat up in bed in bizarre pyjamas

*title of the volume of Welsh hymns by William Williams
published c1750: **Caniadau y Rhai sydd ar y Mor a Wydr**.

Gorgeous - yet another Brighton poem

The summer's here.
Down to the beach
to swim and lounge and swim again.
Gorgeous bodies young and old.
Me too. Just gorgeous. Just feeling good
and happy and so at ease in the world.

And come early evening a red sun setting,
the sea all silky,
small gentle surges along its near still surface.

And later
the new moon hung over the sea,
a stippled band of gold across the black water,
tiger's eye.

I walk home.
The air so soft and warm,
like fur brushing my body.

The dictionary says
"**gorgeous** - adorned with rich and brilliant colours,
sumptuously splendid, showy, magnificent, dazzling."

That's right.

Mirrors

"we create imaginary troubles for ourselves...
we sew our own path with brambles." Flaubert.

in the mirror

        an unknown face

a blank
of flesh, colours, slight movements,
"facial muscles" the words say

something slipping away
                unknown
                    totally unknowable

      "might discover himself not
in the mirror of Narcissus' pool but
in men and upon that arid earth"*

          ...dark hidden motives...

...penetrating clarity...

          ...success through what is small...

...no place to "stay"...

            ...persons quarrelling...

...deep cunning...

           ...repeated deliberation...

Amongst all those words
"conflict means not to love"

A hellish trembling world
or a possible heaven
at the touch or glance of the one you love

Not the lapis lazuli sky, gold leaf stars
way up above beyond the crust
overcrowded heavenly chorus
Not the black red fire world below
in the bowels of the earth
men savagely buggered with long poles
by wretched capering deformed demons

but here   and now

you make it happen   you make it happen

talking in the particular

obvious enough

gulls laugh, screech, and chunter on nearby roofs
morning light glances off the mirror
the sunlight the window the sound of the sea

*Carlo Levi's 1963 Introduction to 'Christ stopped at Eboli'

South Coast

mauve inside of a shell

squealing terns plunging into the sea
hunting   zigzagging
along the edge of the beach

the new bright spring sunshine

these particulars   that hold one

what was it we were trying to say?
were we talking of love?
and other difficult words?

while diving through the glittering light
into out of the sea...

the ochres, whites, greys of the shingle
against the peacock blue-green of the sea
against a pale blue sky

cloudless sparkling air

thoughts and judgements
slide and tumble after each other
untrustworthy untrustworthy
leading nowhere but...

the side of your face
a suntanned hand
a hard glance in the eyes
your mouth

the impossibility of holding onto
anything   anyone
sun sweeps its arc
moon and stars rotate
continually shifting
at night the dull hiss of the surf
sounds constant but fades or pulses
radio static

No?   is this wandering?

something slipping away
a steady reduction of time
notched off

red bands hold the white lighthouse
at the end of the harbour arm
runs and drips of red paint smudge the white edge

sand eels are put on the hook
to catch bass, I'm told

Talking Bab-Ilu

for Anne Stevenson

The words scattered or hidden
since the tower of Babel
and a jealous Jehovah
(get a new job, why don't you?
who needs it? **that** sort of stuff?).

Up and down the ziggurat stairs,
into the skies into the earth.
A gate for gods, not a confusing babble.
The language of trees, of seas,
of winds, plants, and us beasts.

Music after the flood
in the hills and mountains.
As spring comes a young bull
bellows in a high green field.
You stop and listen.

And the other sounds -
the mew of two buzzards up above,
the drumming of water down
over rock slab over rock slab,
my voice talking to myself.

Listening, waiting, drifting
into that space beyond words.
Forgot what I meant to say.
My hands before my eyes.
It can happen.   Clear and bright.

Late Journeys

You think you'll sleep so well tonight
warmed with the glow of feeling precious
to someone else out there.   Can it be?

You don't sleep **that** well,
but what's **that** simple?
Us animals snuffle around so eagerly.

At dusk – coral pink clouds
lined up along the horizon
like mysterious monuments symbolising "Hope".

A weighty full moon hangs over the pier,
silvers the sea, churns our hearts.
Warm silk summer nights.

The orange lights of provincial railway stations.
People walking home, people taking the last train,
shouting across streets, talking on the platform.

It seems all right
whatever may come.

Monuments

Lines of dark trees in a plantation, ivy, bramble

underfoot.

Two charred trunks stand - totems, watchers, uncaring

guardians.

Deeper in the wood a long pit filled with scribbles of

blue light.

On the edge of the wheatfield a forest of slim granite posts

maps a wave.

Naked men broad chested stand fixed on a green path their

faces whitened.

Algae on the stones. Your scent on my hand

my body.

Your body - lines beyond words, warm curve

touch.

Your eyes in the half-light. Your mouth. Lines of a shoulder

dreamed of.

In the viridian undergrowth red stone arches beset a path.

Too obscure?

Heavy metal sections bolted together form

a rough canyon.

Feel it. Cobwebs stretch from rust patina. Still water

in a sexual scoop.

This is not a dream,
I saw all this.
Sweep of your body
in a white room.
Stands of trees.

"So what?" someone snaps   "So what??"

I say

"it's amazing wonderful out there in front of

you."

A neon blue light below the dirt and chalk, a sacred

dusky glow.

Genghis Khan's Hat

Genghis Khan loves his new mauve hat
sent by a feeble emperor far away.
He wears it all the time,
awake and asleep.

Drums and gongs beaten in the encampment.
Wars and skirmishes in the distance.
Coming and going. Fluttering banners.
Horses kick up dust, flying turf.

Among the tent's yellow silk draperies
we're here.
Mr. Mauve Hat is out,
History is out.

The leaves of summer trees
the look in your eyes.
On a distant steppe now
a threadbare hat lying in coarse grass.

Classicism (Satie, Finlay, et Cie..)

Afternoon light slides through a Paris apartment
The white walls and few furnishings
Simple and bare and elegant
Piano music now
The books   the couch

Timeless moment

If you were here
we would stare into each other's eyes
almost frightened so intense the love

"No fear. No harm."
say Chinese sages 3000 years ago

Caravans depart the oasis
Roman mottos grow mossy

"The Temple of Ancient Virtue"
on its knoll   the beech trees turning

Fragments creak in their chains
Grand proclamations chipped and broken   solid stone
Startled birds arpeggio and sweep off into... other trees

The moment   we touch
naked   such a world
overwhelming   so present

A bed scented with cinnamon and vanilla
Dear timeless virtue

Vessel

for Penny and a homage to Chris Drury

Fire in the cairn on a winter mountain
Snow streaked summit   the range of grey
in the ice air

Orange flames waver in a brief home
high above mists and moor, the scattered lochans

You...   I hardly begin to say

The vast landscape we inhabit, we wander in

My mouth stopped with our kisses

To burn with love

Moss and white grass

amongst rocks and boulders

To the south pale rose clouds above the sea
the waves below a dull grey pink at dusk

To launch out
across clawed rock slabs

Thaw Conditions

To get past the concrete slab
the jagged metal
stagnant pools of rust tinted water
a seeming wreck ready to lunge

Traps for the unsuspecting, insects and others

Watched by Security and cashiers

You enter the gates   you enter the wood
thousands of leaves   twigs   blades of grass
millions   countless

Vast landscapes of clouds
move purposefully above us   slowly sailing their way

You could see this so many ways as
our paths weave a braided dance   our bodies too
- but no matter how -
to get clear into the clear
across beyond the fallen pediment
the bolted laws   the grey furrows
through a winter that lasted too many years
it seemed

Tundra turns to surprise   to spring
to sunlight cutting through clouds searching the land
a dam bursting   local destruction   mud and greenery
Banks of herbs and flowers

I gnaw and kiss your shoulder   the smell of your arms
as your head thrown back   at such release
the spring we find

Dante wanders by clasping his **Vita Nuova**
He's miles away   maybe

You dismantle the walls
it takes time   we both know that
The prism's wavering rainbow scatters across the room
Swarming atoms   a delight of differences
alike

An Horatian Ode

"I shall nudge the stars with my lifted head" *

sea sparkle   touch cloud

not denying history   but

never before,   this

the bass music   pitches and springs   just right

tears of such happiness

beauty   the bronze shape shifter

transparency   and you

what you say what you do

in your arms   I cry with joy

like two people in one body

in a well loved landscape

this coast and the hills behind

we find "the daily" amazing

*Horace - **Odes,** first ode, book 1

Beginning of a West Sussex Spell

You lie naked on a mossy bank
The beech woods sigh and hiss in the wind
Soft rain sweeps through and across

No tiger pads by - of course not
No nervous deer skitters by
Your lover covers you from the rain

Now you can dream or watch the sky
your body a masked sun
your face

Tonight

breath white in the street
Tired and clumsy from work
like other citizens   men women in this town

I don't think straight or hear right
I miss what you're saying
My replies not enough

Frost glazes the parks and squares
the fields and valleys beyond
The long winter night outside

Later the sound of your breathing
                    as you sleep beside me
the beauty of your face
                    as you lie asleep beside me
Such precious sharing
our pleasures

Our warm soft night passes

I hear you   you hear me
I hear you   you hear me

I can never write enough to say... I hardly know what I'm trying to say. To describe the gleam in your brown eyes as we lie together? The cinnamon half-light. The clear lines - your eyes, mouth, the outline of your ear, your jaw. The thoughts then... totally without a language, they cut so deep.

Silk Veil

A migrating tribe. The men
advance through the wood,
come out into the clearing.

The majestic pace of the moon
embedded in opal clouds
as it rises above the trees.

Its light catching their rags and faces,
a dull glitter in their eyes.
Threatening or threatened and lost?

A subdued fountain swells up with dark water,
dead leaves slowly spiral beneath its surface.
No messages.   A speechless trust.

Somewhere else - far away -
factories, offices, backyard repair shops
lie empty, locked up for the night,
their dust settling in a near silence.

The advance through to where?
Through the white stone arch,
past polished red granite carved

for our touch and caress now
stood still by the fountain's mirror
as the night passes, fades, as a

brilliant gold rose streaked sun
rises out of the trees
white frost   winter dawn.

As you rise from the bath
water diamonds glitter
in your black ripple hairs.

The History of Science

Beneath the surface   swarming atoms
Landscapes decay sway and thrust
beyond presumption   hardly becalmed
though seemingly so

A man advances his chest sliced with neon
A woman advances as though made of amber
cloaked in gold silk
Pulsing flecks electric blue
Glowing yellows golden browns

Overlap / overlay

Beyond understanding   move into silence
An intensity   large scale

In face
of your sleeping face
Into dream

don't know why

patchwork fields woods
below this blue swaying tower
where we lie craddled
tugged by the wind
in each other's arms

It changes

Great sweeps of loose colours
bright and sexy as you

the sun on your face
this late morning by the sea
how I melt and you dazzle

I dance across the rooftops
never "lonely as a cow"

Beneath the sea   the swaying forests
wave and swirl   undulate like dancers
luminous creatures pulse and build
delicately   so slowly

and not in silence

Lee Harwood, born 1939, lives by the sea in Brighton & Hove. His publications include ...

POETRY

title illegible. Writers Forum. London, 1965; reprinted 1996.
The Man with Blue Eyes. Angel Hair Books, New York, 1966.
The White Room. Fulcrum Press, London, 1968.
Landscapes. Fulcrum Press, London, 1969.
The Sinking Colony. Fulcrum Press, London, 1970
Penguin Modern Poets 19 (with John Ashbery & Tom Raworth)
        Penguin Books, Harmondsworth, 1971.
H.M.S. Little Fox. Oasis Books, London, 1975.
Boston-Brighton. Oasis Books, London, 1977.
All the Wrong Notes. Pig Press, Durham, 1981.
Monster Masks. Pig Press, Durham, 1985.
Crossing the Frozen River: selected poems. Paladin, London, 1988.
Rope Boy to the Rescue. North & South, Twickenham, 1988.
In the Mists: mountain poems. Slow Dancer Press, Nottingham, 1993.

PROSE

Captain Harwood's Log of Stern Statements and Stout Sayings.
        Writers Forum, London, 1973; reprinted 1995.
(with Richard Caddel) Wine Tales: Un Roman Devin
        Galloping Dog Press, Newcastle-upon-Tyne, 1984.
Dream Quilt: 30 assorted stories. Slow Dancer Press, Nottingham, 1985.

TRANSLATIONS

Tristan Tzara - Selected Poems. Trigram Press, London, 1975.
Tristan Tzara - Chanson Dada: selected poems. Coach House
        Press/Underwhich Editions, Toronto, 1987.